GROWING IN LOVE

EFFECTIVE SUPPORT FOR YOUR MARRIAGE

by Michael and Terri Quinn

Handbook for the Married Listening Programme

FAMILY CARING TRUST

First published 1989
by Family Caring Trust
44 Rathfriland Road
Newry
Co. Down
BT34 1LD

Revised edition printed
by Cassidy Printers, 1994

Illustrations and design: Pauline McGrath
Typesetting: Cassidy Printers, Newry
Printing: Universities Press (Belfast) Ltd

ISBN 1 872253 01 6

CONTENTS

———

	page
Getting Started	5
Chapter 1: Listening for feelings	11
Chapter 2: The Decision to love	27
Chapter 3: Dealing with conflict	39
Chapter 4: Letting your marriage grow	53
Course Guidelines	68

GETTING STARTED

'Tom and I were madly in love when we got married, and we wanted to stay in love. We wanted to have closeness and fun, and to have real respect for each other... Maybe that seems like a lot to expect, but we did expect it, we looked forward to it, we didn't want to settle for anything less.'

'I suppose we thought it would just happen. I remember, when we did a pre-marriage course, one of the speakers, a married woman, told us about the disillusion that had hit her, but we honestly didn't think that would happen to us. I suppose our feet weren't on the ground. We didn't realise that we needed special skills for the kind of marriage we wanted — especially for handling our rows and our differences. So it was terrible when things began to go wrong...'

The need for training.

This statement by a young married woman says a lot: people are no longer willing to settle for a dull, routine marriage; they want a great deal from marriage today. The statement also brings out the need for training and support

5

for this kind of marriage. A pre-marriage course can help, of course, but it would seem that the real support needs to come *after* the wedding, when feet are more firmly on the ground. That is what this book and this course are attempting to provide.

Why listening?

In a recent radio interview a woman talked about an incident that happened on the first day of her honeymoon: her husband had objected to the bikini she had just put on for the beach. Suddenly it hit her that this was a side to him that she had never known, nor even suspected. 'Here's a man I don't even know', she had said to herself, 'And only yesterday I vowed to be his wife forever! This is awful!' Happy to say, they are still living happily together years later — and still finding out things about each other which they never suspected!

For a healthy marriage is a union of two separate people who are always changing, always adjusting to what is new in each other - losing each other for a time, and then finding each other.

Communication is the lifeblood of such a marriage. It is often said that marriages break down when people stop talking to one another; it's probably more true that marriages break down when people stop *listening* to one another.

This book (and the programme of which it is a part) looks at ways in which married people can listen better to each other and how they might make space and time for better listening.

Why married women?

Many of the people experiencing this course are married women who attend *without* their husbands. This is because one of the problems about setting up any kind of marriage support in the past was that most men did not seem to be interested. Before the wedding, couples often express enthusiasm for a post-marriage course — they may even come to a once-off reunion — but experience shows that relatively few couples come willingly to a post-marriage course.

That was a problem which one person, Dr. Gleam Powell, faced fairly and squarely in her research. She had set herself to find out what kind of marriage support might be effective and she had no illusions about the difficulty of attracting husbands to courses. What about inviting married women on their own?, she wondered. After all, we bring parents together without their children, to improve the parent-child relationship.

Dr. Powell tried various things with different groups of married women and she measured their success at the end of each course, interviewing not only the wives but also the husbands, and measuring the effect of her courses on the marriage as a whole. Some of the things she tried had little or no real effect, but most of the skills taught in this course are similar to those which she found made a real impact on the marriage.

Does this mean that married women are the only ones who are expected to change, to learn new skills, while their husbands are let off the hook? No. It is very helpful to have both husband and wife on a post-marriage course, and it may be important to see this programme as a step in that process, leaving husbands more *open* to a course for couples. In Dr. Powell's research, many of the husbands subsequently did a post-marriage course *along* with their wives, and our own early findings indicate that about one half of the husbands were open to this. The present course can also be experienced by a group of men without their partners - or by a group of couples, using the separate Leader's Guide.

Flexibility.

This is a flexible programme. It was convenient to speak of 'husband' and 'wife' in these pages, but the course should also be helpful to people who are living together and not married. Moreover, we have tried to allow for the many different styles of marriage that there are. For we all bring

To allow for the many different styles of marriages.

into marriage a thousand and one differences — differences of background, of history, of personality, of work-experience . . . And we enter marriage with different expectations of what it will be like — different couples will want greater or lesser involvement in each other's lives. In this course, then, couples are encouraged to find a pace of growth that suits their unique marriage and to acquire some skills and methods for achieving that. Nor are they expected to use or to agree with everything in the course. Many couples already have a very good relationship and they are not using all the suggestions in this book. What works for one couple may not work for another. That flexibility would seem to be important.

Acknowledgements.

The ideas in this book come from many sources. We owe a great deal to the ideas of Gerard Egan, Chuck Gallagher, Thomas Gordon, Harvey Jackins, David and Vera Mace, Gleam Powell, and Carl Rogers. We would like to thank all the people who helped test the programme throughout Britain and Ireland; also those whom we consulted at various stages about style and content, particularly Gabrielle Allman, Peter Devlin, Philip Leonard, Dick and Dorothy McDonald, Michael and Catherine Molloy, and a number of people from CMAC. We are grateful too, to the Department of Health and Social Services for their grant of £1,000 towards the cost of developing the programme. And a special word of thanks to our very willing and patient secretary, Bernie Magill.

CHAPTER 1: LISTENING FOR FEELINGS

• *'Sometimes I have no feelings of love for Joe at all - I even find myself hating him. And it frightens me.. It frightens me to think that I might go through life saying things like 'I love you' and not meaning them.'*

• *'If [my wife] Ann died, I know I'd feel shattered, but I would also feel a certain relief, a sense of freedom...'*

Don't be afraid of feelings.
There are examples of difficult feelings that can frighten people or make them feel guilty. There are many others. Some people, for example, find it almost impossible to admit that they dislike one of their children, or that they feel jealous. Some men find it difficult to admit, even to themselves, that they have tender 'soft' feelings; some women have the same difficulty in recognising that they feel angry or resentful.

Yet feelings are neither right nor wrong. It may be unpleasant to feel hatred or anger, but it is perfectly okay to feel this way. It is *normal* to feel angry, or hurt, or scared, or whatever, but right and wrong do not arise until I *act* on my feelings — for example by striking someone in anger. Realising this can be a great relief to people who may have spent years judging themselves to be bad because of the way they feel.

11

The importance of listening for feelings.

The point is that feelings change like the wind. They come in all sorts of combinations and strengths and make you a little bit different today to the person you were yesterday. That's one of the things that makes each person so interesting — one of the things, indeed, that makes your husband or wife so interesting. Some marriage counsellors claim that the saddest thing that can happen to a marriage is when the partners take each other so much for granted that they stop noticing the changing feelings, the changing person — when husband and wife think they know each other. Then they stop surprising each other, they become bored with each other, and begin to fall out of love. For they are now only half-listening to one another.

Half-listening. Hearing the words and missing the feelings, missing the ever-changing, unique person behind the words. During this course, you are invited to improve your listening skills, to learn to listen for feelings and to enjoy discovering the richer, deeper and very interesting person you are married to.

How we listen.

So let's begin by considering some ways in which we could improve our listening. Here are ten things people often do when they are not listening (although obviously a lot also depends on the circumstances). Would you like to take half a minute to tick some of these ways in which *you* don't listen:

1. Interrupting.
2. Not looking at the person speaking.
3. Turning your body away.
4. Looking bored or hostile.
5. Folding your arms.
6. Joking.
7. Contradicting.
8. Asking a lot of questions.
9. Offering advice or suggestions.
10. Consoling or reassuring.
    Other ways . . .?

People are sometimes surprised to see numbers eight to ten included here, for it often seems kind to reassure, to console, to ask questions or to offer advice (and there will obviously be a time for all of these). But very often what people most need is the chance to express the thoughts and feelings that are inside them. Questions or advice may actually close them up and make them feel worse. If Christine, for example, is terrified of mice, it can be most unhelpful — even hurtful — to ignore her strong feelings by reassuring her that a little mouse won't harm her.

Improving your listening

However, the emphasis in this course is a positive one; it is important to remember the ways in which we *do* listen well and to build on these. Would you like to tick the following checklist of ten ways in which you *do* listen? Remember that you can tick things you *sometimes* do. It's not necessary to be perfect before you give yourself a tick:

1. Remaining silent.
2. Paying attention and looking.
3. Turning your body, even leaning towards the speaker.
4. Showing care and interest, especially with your eyes.
5. Opening your arms and uncrossing your legs (a closed, protected body can be a sign of a closed mind).
6. Being slow to interrupt by asking questions, joking, offering advice, or trying to console.
7. Occasionally nodding your head or making a helpful comment like 'yes', 'uh-huh', 'mm', 'I see'.
8. Making an occasional comment in a gentle, caring tone of voice.
9. Repeating some of the speaker's words, after a pause, to encourage them to continue.
10. Most important of all, genuinely *caring* and wanting to understand.

Well, how did you get on with that checklist? If your score is on the low side, perhaps you're too hard on yourself. We often tick bad behaviour even if it only occurs some of the time, yet we think we have to be perfect before we give ourselves a tick for good behaviour! And remember that these signs of good listening don't always apply; the most important part of listening is what happens *inside* you — genuinely caring and wanting to understand.

But he says he doesn't know how he feels!

Let's move on now to thinking about feelings. Have you ever been lonely? Have you ever been blue? These words from an old song are two words to describe feelings. There are many others: happy or sad, burdened or carefree, tearful or cheerful, and so on. Yet it's a mistake to expect someone who is confused or upset to be able to find the right words for how they feel. And the same person may be even more confused about the cause of their feelings: 'How can you be lonely when you have such a good husband and such lovely children?' What a silly question — to the loneliness we have just added anxiety and guilt! 'Have you any idea what's causing it?' may not help either. If the person knew what was causing it, they would be more than half way to feeling better, for sometimes the cause is buried so deep in the subconsious that the person *cannot* recognise the cause. So it may not help to ask: *Why* do you feel that way?'

Even when we do know how we feel, it can be difficult to find the right word to describe the feeling. Words may not help. So the art of listening is not only to hear what is being said, but, more importantly, to hear what is *not* being said. To hear in your heart. In marriage, so much is said without words. A touch, a look, (or not looking), can be a language in themselves. In this book we are attempting to keep that language alive — because that can keep a marriage alive.

The skill of active listening.

One very helpful way of listening, which can make a great difference to a marriage, is called *active listening*. For even if you do understand how someone is feeling, it's another matter altogether to get that across to them, to communicate that you understand and to help them to see that you understand. This is precisely what active listening does.

With active listening you listen for your partner's feelings and reflect back in your own words what you hear, checking out that you're on the right wavelength, and at the same time communicating your understanding. For example, John comes in and announces: 'The dog has rooted up the daffodil bulbs again!' Instead of trying to cheer him up: 'Don't worry about it — they can be planted again' or advising him 'I told you not to plant them there — they were too close to the edge', his wife listens for his feelings and says simply: 'That's awfully disappointing. All the time you spent planting them!' There is probably nothing that could have been more helpful to John than this simple communication of her understanding. Similarly, if Barbara comes in angry and hurt because a neighbour has ignored her, it will probably not be helpful if her husband tries to reassure her by pointing out that the neighbour may not have seen her — and it certainly will not help if he joins her in criticising the neighbout: 'The snobby b....!' What might be helpful would be a remark like: 'Mm! She didn't look at you . . . . that can be

The dog has rooted up the daffodil bulbs again.

very hurtful'. In this way he is neither agreeing nor disagreeing with Barbara — just reflecting back what he hears.

Using active listening is not easy at the beginning. Here, for example, is a typical morning scene in the Wilson household.

George: Look, why do you have to take a quarter of an hour to comb your hair every morning.

Linda: I've been here two or three minutes at the most. I wish you wouldn't exaggerate.

George: I'm not exaggerating. You obviously have no idea how long you take. And look, your hairs are all over the place! It's disgusting.

Linda: Look, is there anything else you'd like to complain about while you're at it?

What different approach might Linda have taken in this situation? Well, a sense of humour and a little active listening would have helped; then the conversation might have gone something like this:

George: Why do you have to take a quarter of an hour to comb your hair every morning?

Linda: (lightly) Because I've got half a million hairs — a lot more than someone else I know! Seriously, though, it annoys you that I take so long . . .

15

George: Yes, it does. It's bad enough getting up out of bed without having to wait to get into the bathroom!

Linda: Oh, I see. You're cross about having to wait for the bathroom . . .

Here, Linda didn't react to her husband's grumpiness; instead, she kept things light, listened for his feelings, and reflected back in her own words what she heard.

Active listening may seem like a strange, perhaps artificial, method to use — and it's obviously not something to use all the time — but it doesn't sound at all artificial to someone who has strong feelings. On the contrary, it can give your partner a sense of being listened to and understood, and it's quite a powerful help in drawing a couple together.

What active listening is not.

For most people, active listening is a new skill, and it does take a little bit of getting used to. So let's clarify what it is not.

First of all, active listening (sometimes called 'empathy') is not the same as sympathy. With sympathy I feel sad *for* my partner and I am liable to say something like: 'Don't be upset.' With active listening I am more liable to say: 'That's very upsetting for you.' Active listening is more helpful because it allows my partner to express feelings more freely instead of burying them alive.

Secondly, with active listening we need to be wary of asking questions. Questions can easily distract people and lead them in a different direction. Some people find questions annoying and unhelpful. Much better to respond with a gentle comment like: 'You're worried about...', 'Sounds like you enjoy...', 'You seem to hate...', 'You feel sad about...'. Even a questioning tone in your voice can communicate disapproval, and may cause your partner to close up and say nothing more.

Thirdly, active listening is not *just* a skill or technique. It calls for some skill, certainly, but it also calls for real understanding. Really feeling along with the other, above all *caring*. Without caring, active listening will be false and your partner will quickly recognise the difference.

Doesn't he have to change!

Many of the people who follow this course are married women who attend without their husbands — they would appear to be more open than men in our society to working at relationships. So a common reaction on the first

16

evening is: 'Wait a minute. Why should I have to do all the listening and understanding! What about a little bit of understanding for me! He needs

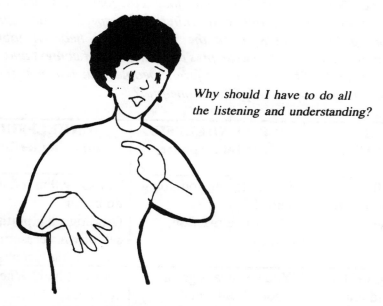

Why should I have to do all the listening and understanding?

to change a lot more than I do!' That's a natural reaction. Yet much experience shows that when you use active listening, when you show genuine caring and understanding for another person, you begin to free that person to change and to be understanding in turn. That is one of the reasons why active listening is so useful in marriage.

And there is an added advantage — improving your listening is probably the single most effective personality improvement you can make. You can be a better person, more valued by all your friends, when you develop your listening skills.

GETTING IN TOUCH

To become more aware of how you listen, the suggestion is that you take a few minutes entirely on your own to tick any of the ten ways in which your listening is weak (under the heading 'How we listen' in Chapter One). Then read on and tick any of the ten ways in which you do listen well in the following section 'Improving our listening'.

TABLE 1: HOW'S MY LISTENING?

The remarks below are divided into four categories. All the helpful remarks are examples of active listening - the speakers are showing understanding by reflecting back the feelings they hear. A table, of course, simplifies things - the examples are taken out of context and might be expressed quite differently by different people. But can you see why each remark is considered helpful or unhelpful?

OPENING REMARK	VERY UNHELPFUL Hurtful response	UNHELPFUL Ignoring feelings
'Don't tell me you've spent all the money!'	'I'd like to see you doing better!' (Defensive reaction; hurtful.	'I'm sorry. I'm trying to do better.' (Apologising, putting self down, reassuring, not hearing feelings.)
'Not tonight. I've got a headache.'	'You've always got a bloody headache!' (Making little of the feelings. Putting down.)	'Oh! Is it bad? When did you get it?' (Questions often close people up.)
(Arriving home) 'What a lousy day!'	'Don't bother telling me - mine was terrible too!' (Wants own needs met.)	'Would you feed the baby while I get the potatoes on.' (Ignoring feelings.)
'What am I going to do with that child!'	Partner continues to watch television. (No communication, not even looking at speaker.)	'She's just in bad form. Let her alone; she'll be okay in the morning.' (Solving problems or offering advice is still ignoring the feelings.)

HELPFUL **Hears surface feelings**	VERY HELPFUL **Hears underlying feelings**
'You're angry about the way I spend money.' (Recognises the feelings.)	'You're anxious about the way the money seems to disappear.' (Recognises the feelings *underlying* the anger.)
'That's tough. Must be awful!' (Shows some understanding	'Mm. You have had a lot of pressures and tension lately.' (Speaker is liable to open out and admit further feelings, including feelings about sex.)
'You're very tired' (Shows you have at least *heard* how other feels.)	'Sounds like it's been tough for you... You're feeling shattered.. (Understanding what might be *behind* the tiredness.)
"You're upset with her.' (Recognising the surface feelings can be a good place to start communicating.)	'You're feeling helpless about her... You've a sense of failure as a parent..' (Can gradually help partner to recognise underlying feelings - often about self

CASE STUDIES (Alternative to listening to the cassette tapes)

Form groups of three, read the following three examples, and see if you can decide together which column in Table 1 each reaction belongs to - Unhelpful or Very Unhelpful. Give reasons for your choice.

1. Jack: 'That child is getting completely out of hand. She goes to bed late every night, and of course she can't get up in the morning!'
   Daphne: **Well, what do you expect? You don't exactly give her much of an example!**

2. Julie: 'I'm out all day working and, when I come home, what do I have to face? - more pressure! It's just endless!'
   Gary: **Well, the bills have to be paid, Julie, so you can't afford to stop working.**

3. Sam: 'You know, I'm next in line if anyone else is made redundant.'
   Beth: **Don't worry about it, Sam, it'll probably never happen. Anyway, if we have to, we'll face that when it comes.**

Remaining in the groups of three, you could move on to chat about the following two situations:

• Sandra speaks to her husband Clive in frustration: 'You're not going off again to play football! This is the third time this week!'
How do you think Sandra is feeling here? Decide what might be a typical or unhelpful reaction from her husband. And what might be a helpful approach for him to take? Can you think of what he might say to use active listening and help her to feel understood?

• Jack arrives home from work, tired. The first thing he says to his wife is: 'Get that cat off my chair! It shouldn't be let into the house!... Hairs all over the place!..'
How do you think Jack is feeling - behind the grumpy front? And how might his wife respect both herself and him? Bearing in mind that it's good to respect your partner's space and not zone in immediately on their deeper feelings, how might she use active listening?

PLANS FOR NEXT WEEK

Here is something to practise with your partner before the next session: Take a little time together (3-5 minutes each), taking turns to listen to each other without any interruption. Choose a time when you'll be relaxed and free from distractions — it's usually important to time yourselves so that your chat isn't too long and doesn't become a burden to one or both of you. When one person has spoken, the other sums up briefly in their own words what they've just heard. You might ask your partner to do this exercise with you, explaining that you're anxious to learn to become a better and more understanding listener. Enjoy the chat. You will learn a lot about yourself and about your partner and you'll be developing important communication skills — but don't expect overnight changes.

Here are some topics to get started. Choose them in any order you like, or choose different topics if you wish. It would be great if you could get through all of them, but do try this exercise at least once before the next session:

1. My best memories of meeting you and going out with you before we got married.
2. What I remember now about our honeymoon.
3. My best memories of our early marriage.
4. My childhood — happy or unhappy? Some of my best and worst memories.
5. My clearest memories of my parents when I was a child?
6. An incident/time when I was terribly upset/sad/lonely.

For various reasons, some partners won't be open to this exercise. If not, you might introduce one of these topics casually and chat about it informally. It's still possible to practise and improve your listening skills, even with someone who is unco-operative. And you'll make extra progress if you also practise listening with your children and friends.

TIPS FOR GETTING ALONG BETTER

● You can't force your partner to talk. Some people find it very difficult to express themselves. They may not know how they're feeling when they're upset. They may need space and time alone by themselves. So just be satisfied to feel with them, to bide your time patiently, and not to push, at times not even to ask "What's happening?" You can practise listening and caring even when your partner is not talking.

● *There are a number of different ways to communicate that you're listening and to encourage your partner to say more. Here are four key ways:*
*1. **Take the time.** The more relaxed you are, the more you can hear what's being said. That usually means setting aside what you're doing, turning towards your partner, sitting down to be at the same level, not fidgeting but giving your fullest attention, looking, nodding, sometimes touching, showing with your face and with your eyes that you understand and that you care. Research indicates that our body positions, our gestures, our tone of voice, communicate more than 90% of our message, while our words alone account for less than 10%.*
*2. When there is a pause, you might **repeat a few words** that seemed to be important in what has just been said.*
*3. **Listen for the feelings** and reflect them back in your own words: 'That was very annoying for you'; 'You must have been terribly embarrased'; 'Sounds like you're at the end of your tether'.*
*4. When your partner has finished speaking, it's not enough to say: 'I understand how you feel'. It usually helps to **sum up in your own words** what you've heard, including the feelings, checking out that you have understood. This feedback can often surprise the person who has spoken — it clarifies, puts things together, makes them aware of feelings they didn't even suspect.*

● Immature people often blame each other for their feelings — 'You make me feel nervous, guilty, bad...' But it's not your partner's fault that you feel the way you do; it is because of the kind of person you are. Accepting that you're responsible for your own feelings is a mature, adult decision.

● *There are three stages to active listening: 1. The most difficult stage — switch off your own anxieties and concerns, and make a conscious decision to listen in a caring way. 2. Listen for the feelings behind the words — get in touch with the person rather than the topic (s)he is talking about. Ask yourself: What's going on inside him/her? What exactly is (s)he feeling right now? 3. Reflect back in your own words the feelings you hear. People often begin to learn the skill of active listening by simply saying: 'You're feeling... because...', e.g. 'you're feeling sad because you have to go back to work tomorrow'.*

● It can be fascinating to notice what happens when you allow your partner to speak without any interruptions — without even a question. People can sometimes be led off on a different track by questions instead of continuing to talk about what really matters to them.

● *Don't expect a partner to be too positive when you arrive home after a session of this course. They may not ask you how you got on — they may be quite dismissive of the whole thing. If so, it is best to ignore their words, if possible, and to be sensitive to their feelings; they may be quite nervous about you doing a marriage course, or they may wonder if you are talking to others about them.*

● Practice is vital if you are to learn these skills and enrich your marriage. Your partner may be more open to it if you mention that it is to help *you* to be a better listener (which is quite true). However, you can't force a partner to talk, so, if they object, it may be possible to practise similar exercises with a friend or with one of your children.

COMMENTS
AND
REACTIONS

The statements in the 'Comments and Reactions' section after each chapter were all made by people following the four-week course on Married Listening.

"Doing the exercise convinced me — it was great to feel you had someone's whole attention. I had a sense of being really listened to."

"My husband would scream if I answered him like that! It's artificial. I'd look stupid."

"I like it — it's a civilised way to treat each other — it shows respect."

"I've discovered I'm not as good a listener as I thought I was. In fact, I haven't been really listening to people at all."

"I've no idea what my husband works at during the day — it's just something he never talks to me about, and he doesn't even expect me to be interested. It never struck me until now that I might be missing out a bit — I really don't know about his worries or pressures, even what he enjoys working at."

"For hundreds of years women were expected to be subservient. Now at last we're beginning to recognise that we've got rights and that we're equal. So I'm not so sure when I hear all this talk about listening to husbands. We need to be listened to and understood even more!"

"When I came home from the first session I was annoyed that my husband didn't ask me anything about it. Later I picked up that he was quite nervous that I was doing a course on marriage, and he thought I was going to try to change him. I think it's important to explain to your husband that the purpose of the course is to change yourself."

"I've been trying to change Gerry since we got married, but I suppose his background and mine are so different and I realise I haven't really been listening to how *he* sees things."

"I decided to do this course because I was desperate — Joe treats me well, but there's almost no communication between us. He doesn't see anything wrong, but I just can't live like this."

"I've seen miracles worked just by listening. When someone listens to you and understands what you're going through, it's like a weight being lifted off your shoulders and you feel lighter and freer."

Choose a time when you'll be relaxed and free from distractions.

CHAPTER 2 — THE DECISION TO LOVE

Pete had spent hours putting up the clothes line in the backyard. He had dug the hole and mixed the concrete himself. Now at last the line was up. True, it wasn't dead straight, but it was quite adequate. He had a real sense of achievement.

When he came in through the back door, his wife Alice was at the window, surveying the line. She greeted him with: 'It's crooked. Look. Slanted to the left. Why didn't you get a handyman when I told you! But no, you wouldn't listen to anybody!'

The damage criticism does.
No doubt Alice did not mean to hurt or discourage Peter. She probably did not even think her remark was hurtful, but her approach is a discouraging one. She is discouraging Peter by finding fault.

Criticising and discouraging those closest to us is all too common in a family and in a marriage. It is very natural, of course, to want to correct your partner, but criticism is just not an effective way to do that. None of us likes to be nagged at, scolded, lectured, bossed or shamed. All these

27

ways of criticising can do damage. They discourage, they undermine a partner's self-confidence, and they can gradually nibble away at a couple's love for each other, leaving bitterness and disillusion instead.

Criticism without words.

Let's look at another example. Brendan and Carmel have two pre-school children, and Carmel has given up her job to be at home with them. It's hard. She misses her friends. She misses getting out. And she misses the sense of being worthwhile that she had when she was earning money. It is particularly bad at the moment because both of the children have had temperatures all day and she has been rushed off her feet. The house is upside-down, there are toys and clothes scattered over the floor, the beds are unmade, and one child is screaming.

Her husband arrives home. She would love a little bit of understanding, someone to listen to her, but Brendan steps over the toys and says: 'Dinner not ready?'

He has no idea. She can see annoyance written across his face. He doesn't have to say: 'You're a lousy manager' but she gets the message. In fact, he doesn't say anything more — he just walks out of the room, closes the door sharply behind him, and slumps in front of the television.

Criticism does not have to be expressed in words. It can come across in someone's tone of voice, in the expression on their face, in how they behave, even in the way they close the door! Brendan had said nothing critical, but Carmel probably feels a lot more discouraged and alone now because of the criticism she experienced. Perhaps the most discouraging thing of all was the lack of understanding or caring, the lack of listening.

Looking for efforts or improvements.

Emphasising the negative does not usually help people to change, and it obviously does not help to strengthen a marriage. Emphasising the positive, on the other hand, is so much more encouraging and helpful. In the first example, Pete had put a great deal of effort and time into the task of putting up the clothes line. Instead of focusing on the one flaw, the one thing she did not like, Alice might have been so much more encouraging if she had been on the lookout for the positive. Not that there was any need to go into ecstacies about the clothes line. All she had to say was something like: 'Thanks Pete — I'll not know myself now with the clothes line so handy' (emphasising the effect, the *improvement*.). Or 'You must be exhausted.

Thanks for taking the time.' (emphasising the *effort* made). A cup of tea or a glass of beer might have been even more encouraging — for actions can speak louder than words!

In the second example, with the house so untidy and the dinner not made, Brendan might have thought that there *was* nothing positive for him to encourage. But true encouragement does not look for results or success or achievements — it just looks out for any efforts or improvements. Carmel had tried hard — she had done her best all day (very few people, in fact, do not do their best, given their circumstances), and Brendan would have done well to have recognised that. If he had said something like: 'I can see you've had a tough day. You must be at the end of your tether', he would have been showing her some understanding and recognising the efforts she had been making. That might have been very encouraging for Carmel, and she would have felt less alone. Obviously, deeds might again have been more encouraging than words if Brendan had cheerfully got into action and shown his consideration by attending to the children or to the dinner.

So let's look now at what encouragement is *not* in order to understand more clearly what it does involve.

Encouragement is not the same as praise.

Encouragement is not the same as praise. Praise, as we have seen, tends to emphasise success or achievement. That is okay — people who encourage will naturally be *happy* about your achievement and congratulate you. But they do not wait until you are successful before they encourage you; they are aware of the *effort* you have made anyway.

Secondly, praise tends to exaggerate — to be too lavish: 'You're fantastic!' That often leaves the other person feeling embarrassed rather than encouraged. Encouragement is usually quite low-key and casual, but it gives you a sense of being appreciated, of your effort being noticed. Encouragement says: 'Mm. That was hard work.' Rather than: 'You're the best worker I know!'

Thirdly, praise tends to make general statements: 'That's a terrific job!': 'You're a brilliant cook!' The other person can end up wondering what standard you're using and perhaps feeling uncomfortable about having to live up to that standard. Encouragement, on the other hand, makes personal statements; it usually emphasises the *effect* of your action on *me*: 'I like that.': 'Thanks. I enjoyed that dinner.': 'I love your hair like that.' Personal statements sound more natural and more genuine.

Much more than mere words.

Some people think that encouragement is really a matter of saying the right *words*. But the truth is that encouragement is more a matter of how we think than of what we say; genuine encouragement flows from a cheerful, friendly, positive frame of mind.

It comes as a surprise to many people that this positive frame of mind can be practised and learnt. We can *choose* to be positive. This frame of mind can be developed, for example, by deciding first thing every morning, even before you get out of bed: 'This morning I'm going to be cheerful at breakfast.' or 'Today I'll look for two good things about my partner — different from what I appreciated yesterday.' A good start like this can set the right mood for the rest of the day — just as a poor start, acting grumpy and miserable, can do damage and set the opposite mood.

Encouragement and active listening.

But what happens when there seems to be nothing special in your partner to appreciate? — your wife nags a lot, or your husband refuses to communicate, is irritable and moody.

Love is a decision.

This is where active listening comes in. For active listening is another form of encouragement that goes far beyond words. When you stop and listen and begin to understand the pain and depression behind the nagging, or the discouragement and fear behind the gruff front, then you can begin to appreciate the *person*. It is not necessary to pretend that your partner has qualities which are not there. All you have to do is listen and communicate that you understand.

Can you remember a time when someone set everything else aside and made time for you — when they showed you that they were listening and they understood? You have the power to encourage your partner like that when you use active listening. A remark like: 'You're feeling rotten. That's awful', can bring new light and hope to your partner's eyes. Using active listening is one of the most loving and most encouraging things you can do for each other.

Love is a decision.

We have already seen that actions can be much more encouraging than words. Little acts of consideration can be *most* encouraging — a hug, even a touch that says: 'I notice you', an unexpected cup of tea or coffee that says: 'I think I know how badly you're feeling', helping each other in the home, speaking gently, giving breakfast in bed, buying a surprise gift, making time for a chat, generally showing thoughtfulness and day-to-day friendship. All these things can communicate understanding and they help a partner feel less alone. Words of encouragement without such acts of consideration can sound very empty.

This kind of loving has nothing to do with being syrupy or 'smoochy'. As we will see, a healthy marriage must leave room for arguments, conflict, and the expression of tensions. In every marriage there will be times when the partners do not have loving feelings for each other, when they may feel positive dislike, even hatred for each other. As we saw in the last chapter, these feelings, though unpleasant, are neither right nor wrong until they're acted upon. It is important to realise this, for some people think their marriage is in trouble when they have no feelings of love. They overlook the fact that love is not just a feeling; love is a decision — a decision, for example, to be considerate and friendly, thoughtful and encouraging, even when positive feelings are missing. Experience shows that positive feelings usually follow quite quickly once we make that decision to look for the good and to do something thoughtful.

To sum up then. Truly encouraging people are usually on the look-out for the positive. They do not look for success or achievements; rather they are happy to look for small improvements ('That helps me') or efforts ('Thanks for trying anyway'). They usually express their appreciation in simple _personal_ terms: ('I like the way you did that') rather than in general terms. And their encouragement flows from a friendly, positive frame of mind - which often depends on a _decision_ to be positive. Such people often breathe new life into their partners, and love gradually deepens and grows in their marriages.

GETTING IN TOUCH

How often do you make these (or similar) remarks? Put a tick beside any of them that remind you of something you do or say. Remember that criticism makes it more difficult for people even to make an effort or to improve; it tends to undermine and destroy confidence. Praise, on the other hand, may be okay at times, but encouragement tends to be simpler, less exaggerated, more personal. Praise can be hard to live up to, whereas encouragement helps people to have more belief and confidence in themselves.

DISCOURAGEMENT - 1. You're stupid/selfish.. (name-calling). 2. Criticising/ putting your partner down. 3. Blaming, nagging, finding fault. 4. Not noticing efforts. 5. Not making allowances or being understanding. 6. Being indifferent, cold or moody.

PRAISE - 1. You're terrific! 2. You're a fantastic (woman/ man/ cook!...) 3. You're so kind/ thoughtful... 4. Thanks, darling. You're an angel.

ENCOURAGEMENT - 1. Thanks. That's a help. 2. I like the way you.. 3. I think you've got better at.. 4. Thanks for trying anyway. 5. Being cheerful and warm. 6. Noticing efforts. 7. Performing little unexpected acts of thoughtfulness. 8. Active listening and understanding.

TABLE 2 — HOW ENCOURAGING ARE YOU?

PRAISE — Usually exaggerated and general (not personal). Looks for success and achievement.	CRITICISM — Discouraging and hurtful; looks for mistakes and faults. Often exaggerates or uses sarcasm.	ENCOURAGEMENT — usually personal (how I feel). Looks for efforts made and effects/improvements.
Sarah: *You're a super dad for the children.*	*You don't think about the children — you don't even see them!*	*I'm glad you took the children out. You can see they loved it.*
Bill: *You're wonderful with people!*	*You spend too much time with those friends.*	*I like the way you dealt with her. She can be terribly awkward, but you were firm with her without being rude.*
Imelda: *What a fantastic job you've done on that door. You're great.*	*The handle has come off again! Typical of one of your patch-up jobs!*	*That was hard work — it took up a lot of your time, but it makes things a lot easier for me. Thanks.*
Arthur: *You're a really beautiful woman!*	*All you seem to think of is dressing up.*	*Thanks for dressing up. You look much better. I love that dress on you.*
Jean: *Oh well, you'll win the next time.*	*There's worse things than losing. You spend too much time playing darts anyway.*	*I like the way you keep trying.*
Maurice: *You're a terrific driver!*	*The light's green! Are we parked!*	*I feel very relaxed when you're driving.*

33

CASE STUDIES (Alternative to listening to the cassette tapes)

1. Form groups of three, and decide which column in Table 2 each of the following remarks might belong to. Give reasons for what you think. For example, how might you feel if your partner said them to you? Be open to others in your group who might feel differently.

- 'You know, John - you're one of the best-looking men in this country!'
- I don't know where you get the patience to talk to her, Amanda, but I like the way you make time for people.
- 'Hurry up! Do you have to take all day?'
- 'Are you still talking about the time you went to the States!'
- 'You're terrific! Just brilliant!'
- 'Oh, grow up!
- Thanks for putting the bin out - I hate doing that job.
- 'Don't cry, darling. I still love you.'
- 'I like that sweater on you - nice and cuddly.'
- 'Thanks for dressing up. It makes me feel more special going out.'
- 'You're a bitch!'
- 'You're shattered....You look like you've had a tough day...'

2. Many people think that the greatest way to encourage is to listen and show understanding. How might you encourage your partner to talk and feel understood in the following situations?
- Your partner has been made redundant, (or passed over for promotion).
- Your partner has become quiet and withdrawn recently.
- Your partner has recently been feeling angry and frustrated with one of the children.

PLANS FOR NEXT WEEK

Here are a few more topics for practising your active listening skills. Make sure to have at least one special chat with your partner during the week. Allow your partner to speak for three to five minutes without interruption, and briefly repeat back to them in your own words what you heard — especially the feelings. Then it's your turn to talk. If anything 'difficult' crops up, it is usually best not to discuss it there and then, but to postpone it. Next week we'll be looking at effective ways of dealing with problem areas. Choose any topic, not necessarily in the order in which they are here:

1. Some of the times when I felt very happy — either recently or long ago.
2. The biggest worry in my life at the moment.
3. What was really going on inside me today — what I enjoyed, what worries or pressures I had.
4. What I'm looking forward to most at present. How I feel about the future — my own, my partner's, the future in general.
5. Some of the times in my life when I really appreciated you and felt close to you were...
6. Some of the thoughts and feelings that were going through me today.

First thing in the morning, before you get out of bed, you can decide to start off the day cheerfully. See if you can think of one little surprise, one thoughtful act, to do for your partner each day — a hug, making an unexpected cuppa, noticing something good about your partner and mentioning it, making time for a chat, being cheerful and showing friendliness when you don't feel like it, using active listening when feelings are strong... There's probably nothing you can do for your partner so encouraging as making time to sit down and listen. Notice, too, how you feel after doing something thoughtful. Many people who are in bad form claim that moving out of themselves and doing something considerate for another begins to make them feel better about themselves.

TIPS FOR GETTING ALONG BETTER

● Encouragement is a way of life, a mentality. It is not merely a question of what we say but of how we think and how we express that in our words, our looks, our touch, our smile, our listening, our actions.

● *Keep on the lookout for the good, for things to appreciate, in your partner, for there is a great deal more good than bad in everyone, and far more strengths than flaws. Experts on the spiritual life claim that the secret of inner peace and happiness is to be grateful, so you will benefit as much as anyone else when you appreciate the good in others.*

● Here are some ways of cultivating a positive frame of mind.
1. Set small targets: 'I'll be cheerful at breakfast' rather than 'I'll be friendly all day today'.
2. Plan positive things: 'I'll hug my husband when I come home from work' rather than 'I won't nag'. Negative resolutions can actually suggest negative behaviour.
3. Keep going — remind yourself of your successes rather than be discouraged by your failures.

● *Think about the following statement: 'Efforts and improvements increase when they're noticed. You could try repeating it to yourself until it sinks in. Notice how true it is in your own experience. For when you believe in the power of encouragement, encouraging will tend to come more naturally to you.*

● When you want to mention something you appreciate, it helps to make a *personal* statment: 'I like the way you were able to put everything aside and make time for her.' 'I felt accepted right away when you said that.' 'I love to see that little twinkle in your eyes — it cheers me up.' 'I'm impressed by the way you handled that...'

● *It can be very discouraging to live with tension and bad feeling. Making up, saying sorry, giving and asking forgiveness are all good ways of clearing the air, and of encouraging.*

● Touch can be very encouraging in a marriage. An unexpected hug, a gentle touch, caressing your partner in a way that eases tension and communicates understanding — these can all be most encouraging.

● *Active listening is one of the best ways of all to encourage another person, tor it helps them to feel cared about, listened to and understood.*

● Actions speak louder than words. See if you can plan a few unexpected acts of kindness and thoughtfulness for your partner — little decisions to love, little surprises. You'll probably find that they help you to feel better as well.

COMMENTS
AND
REACTIONS

"On the first evening you said that my husband would change when I changed, but I honestly didn't believe that. I had a sinking feeling that I was going to have to do all the changing on my own. But it is working. I've done a lot of thoughtful little things for Vincent and it has made a difference — we're getting on better. And moving out of myself seems to leave me happier as well."

"Your examples of criticism don't go far enough — people can be even more cruel to each other in subtle, educated ways. Being superior and sarcastic, for example — and not listening. That's criticism too."

"What hit me most was hearing that love was a decision — that sometimes the feelings will be there and sometimes they won't. I find that a great relief."

"Life isn't like that — people don't go round being sweet and smiley to each other. Yuk! I wouldn't *want* Bob to treat me like that."

"We're more patient with each other — gentler, I suppose..."

"I like it when he says 'You feel... because...' The 'because' really shows that he's listening."

"I always had the impression that she disapproved of me drinking, so it meant a lot to me when she handed me a beer last night. It changed the whole atmosphere."

"I was glad you said it wasn't a question of words. I think it's just a question of being thoughtful — putting yourself in the other's shoes and thinking: 'What would they like?' But that doesn't come naturally — a lot of people just think about themselves today. They just never think of others."

"Criticising someone isn't the only way to get his back up. Giving orders is far worse. Yesterday I said: 'Sean, the clothes need to be taken in off the line, and the dishes have to be dried. Which would you rather do?' Giving someone a choice is a great way to get them to co-operate."

CHAPTER 3: DEALING WITH CONFLICT

Stephen:	(shouting): Where the hell were you? Do you realise this child has been screaming for half an hour!
Eileen:	You know I was shopping! And there's no need to shout!
Steven:	(still shouting): I'm not shouting! — but the child is *hungry* You didn't think of *feeding* her before you left?!
Eileen:	Wait a minute! Why didn't you feed her!! Why should it all depend on me!! You're her father and it's time you started acting like a father!
Stephen:	This is great! Blame me — that's it. I walk up and down for half an hour with a screaming child and then you come in and attack *me*. You're just like your mother — and you get more like her every day!
Eileen:	Oh shut up. What do you expect me to do — give you a medal? You depress me!
Stephen:	I depress you! I depress *you!* And what the hell effect do you think *you* have on *me*?
Eileen:	I couldn't care less what effect I have on you... (going out of the room and slamming the door).

I'm not shouting

A good row does no harm.

This is a fairly normal row for Eileen and Stephen. They claim to be very real with each other when they are angry or upset and they believe that a good row does no harm to their marriage.

They are quite right. A good row does no harm to a marriage. It can be a very healthy thing. Some brothers and sisters fight and squabble endlessly — yet they can be each other's best friends. A good row is even something to be encouraged. 'If you never have rows,' says a recent pamphlet from Relate, 'Your marriage is probably not worth rowing about, or else one of you always gives in to the other. A good row can often clear the air and help to get to the root cause of things that have been festering for some time.'

A *good* row, that is. But the row above is not really a good one. Let's see why.

First of all, neither Stephen nor Eileen stuck to the point. It's important, of course, to decide what the point is — rows often start over minor details that are merely the last straw in a build-up of tension. In this case, the couple probably need to talk about sharing responsibility for the baby if they want to avoid having very similar rows occurring again and again in the future. Not only did they not stick to the point, but Eileen actually walked out in the middle of their fight — something which shouldn't happen in a 'good row'.

Secondly, they showed little or no respect for each other — there was a lot of criticism and putting down of each other. We saw in the last chapter how hurtful these remarks can be; a marriage cannot stand up to this kind of abuse for long without a good deal of damage being done.

And there certainly was no listening or understanding. The fight was not constructive; it was destructive.

Smoothing things over.

Before we examine what a constructive fight is, let's just look at another example. Pauline and Trevor get along very smoothly. They avoid talking about anything that might cause tension between them. They cannot remember ever having had a row. To avoid any conflict they have also worked out different areas of responsibility over the years. Trevor has his work, his friends, sports, the garden; Pauline has her family, her friends, a part-time job as a nurse. Pauline buys the household items and Trevor never questions her wisdom; Trevor decides about major items of expenditure like a car.

It may be a good idea to have different areas of responsibility, of course. But in this case the problem is that Trevor and Pauline skirt each other, brushing differences under the carpet and pretending they are not there; they have created no-go areas in their marriage — he won't question her decisions about the children, even if he has to bury alive his feelings of irritation; she won't question his control of money, no matter how unfree and crippling she may find it; neither of them want to discuss their feelings about sex, although their sexual relationship is far from satisfactory.

In some ways, Pauline and Trevor would appear to have a very good marriage — and it certainly has its strengths. But something very important is missing — communication about their differences, especially communication of feelings. It's a pity they don't have an occasional row that might clear the air and give them a fresh start. In a good marriage, a couple usually learn to respect each others differences, to see differences as good, rather than to avoid them. In this marriage, all may be sweet and polite on the surface, but the marriage has stopped growing. They need to begin to talk about their tensions if life and growth and love are to come back into their marriage.

Other unhelpful ways of dealing with tensions.

There are other ways of dealing with tensions that are not helpful. Letting one partner make all the decisions. Giving each other the ice-cold treatment

Giving each other the ice-cold treatment.

or the silent treatment for hours, even days, on end. Raking up the past, in fact raking up anything that seems to offer ammunition for throwing at each other in the heat of a row. Talking negatively *about* each other to family and relatives, perhaps especially to mother — instead of talking *to* each other.

So what can a couple do? How can they handle their differences, their different approaches to life, their different values, ideas, feelings, in ways that respect each other and that strengthen their marriage?

Deciding to face up to problems.

Well, firstly, it may need to be repeated that a row can do a lot of good. Instead of sidestepping or walking on eggs around each other, pretending that the differences don't exist — and perhaps letting the tension build up until it explodes — it helps to bring the tension out into the open and talk it out. Okay, maybe your anger will get the better of you, and you won't say things as gently as you would like to, but it's healthier for you and for your marriage to take that risk than to continue to grin and bear it.

See if you can postpone talking until you find a time that suits you both — though that's not always possible. Maybe wash the dishes, sweep the yard, or go for a walk, until tempers have cooled down a bit. Look for a time when you're not too tired (so not last thing before going to bed!), and when there aren't too many distractions around. After the children have been settled, for example, and maybe even with the phone off the hook.

Starting with active listening.

Secondly, it is a great help to use active listening. If you begin by trying to understand your partner's point of view, and then summing up what you have heard, you are showing real respect for their differences and you will take the steam out of the row. It will then be much easier to discuss the matter reasonably and without getting too heated. This applies when you sit down to talk out a problem, but it also applies to problems that crop up at any time.

For active listening is also very useful in the heat of the moment, when a partner has strong feelings. If you only hear the surface feelings, like anger, you can start arguing; but once you become aware of the deeper feeings, the confusion or disappointment or worry underlying the anger, you can begin to melt and be drawn together again. In the example at the beginning of this chapter, when Eileen arrived home to find an angry Stephen trying to cope with a screaming child, she would have done well to have begun by recognising that Steven was very upset. If she had said something like: 'I'm sorry, Stephen, you must be up the walls!' Stephen might have begun to feel better, although it would probably have taken him some time to calm down.

Personal statements — or I-messages.

Active listening recognises a *partner's* feelings in a tense situation, but what about *your* feelings? They may be very strong too! What can you do when you are very upset about a problem, or when you feel hurt or disillisioned with your partner? In this case, the most helpful approach may be to give what Dr Thomas Gordon calls an 'I-message', that is, a simple, personal message, not blaming, not criticising, but telling your partner how you feel and why: 'I feel weary when I find your socks on the bedroom floor because I seem to spend so much time tidying.'; 'I feel terribly embarrassed when you talk about me like that in front of my mother because I know she can't cope with it.'; 'I feel quite distant from you when you spend so much time watching T.V. because I've a sense of not being important to you.'; 'When you scold the children like that, I feel really depressed because I want you to be good friends, and I can see them just tuning you out'; 'When you drive so fast, I get very frightened and nervous because it reminds me of the accident I was in.'

Note that there is a fixed way of giving I-messages: 'I feel... when... because...' It is not necessary to follow this formula too strictly, but it's useful for *practising* I-messages until you're more at ease with them.

Note, too, that I-messages tend to express *underlying* feelings like hurt, disappointment, or helplessness rather than the much less helpful *surface* feelings like anger or hatred. In that way, an I-message makes you vulnerable and helps your partner to listen to you; it doesn't attack. It is a very powerful and effective way of dealing with things that bother you personally — but it is only by *giving* I-messages that you will learn what is effective for you — some of the examples above might not be effective at all with *your* partner, because each couple is different.

Finding long-term solutions.

These skills, then — saying how you see things and how you feel, together with active listening — lay the foundation for effective problem-solving. They enable a couple to talk things out in a constructive way, to get to the core of a problem, to their frustrations, their needs, etc. This can lead to long-term solutions rather than to unsatisfactory patching up.

But how does a couple get from the point of talking out a problem to finding a satisfactory solution? Table Three which follows shows six stages for solving a problem that have proven helpful to a great many people. It won't be necessary to go through all these stages with minor problems, but it can be a very good idea to start with minor problems for practice. Just bear in mind that the most important stage — and the most important problem-solving skill — is active listening. So it's always worth spending extra time on stage one, making sure that you have understood your partner's feelings and that (s)he has a sense of being understood.

Stage two, telling your own feelings and getting your partner to sum up what they have heard, is also important so that you meet as two equals with respect for each other's differences. The remaining four stages help to bring you from understanding through to a specific agreement. There are no rules of course, about how a husband and wife should share out their responsibilities in the home. That depends on each individual couple. The important thing is that you do not assume that the man does certain traditional things and the woman others, but that you talk out these responsibilities and come to some agreement on them.

But what if your partner is not willing to talk, to communicate? What if (s)he just huffs? Well, it's best not to force the issue or to push. When one of you is very deeply hurt, it may take some time before you're ready to talk — we've already seen the value of postponing discussion until a more suitable time. But it is strongly recommended that you never go to sleep at night without some form of reconciliation, even something like: 'I'm too tired and upset now to talk it out, but I want you to know before I go to sleep that I want to talk this out and be close to you again.' Remember, too, that understanding and active listening is usually the best way to soften a partner who refuses to talk. In the next chapter, we will be looking at some further ways that may help.

Let's sum up then. Tensions, and the conflict that arises from them, can do a good deal of harm to a marriage when they are not handled properly. But tensions and conflict can also offer great opportunities for growing in our respect and appreciation for each other's differences and for deepening our love for one another. Couples usually look forward to sharing their lives together as best friends and growing in love and respect for each other right through their lives. That is not an impossible romantic dream; in fact, dealing well with crises, with problems, with conflict and anger, can help make the dream a reality.

TABLE 3 — DEALING WITH PROBLEMS

It is suggested that you postpone talking through a problem until a suitable time — a time when neither of the partners is under strain. It helps to have a relaxed setting when you can be physically close, able to look at each other and be sensitive to each other.

	Unthinking approach.	1. Start with listening.	2. Tell how you feel.
	Attack, blame your partner, accuse, make hurtful remarks.	Make sure your partner feels understood before moving on to the next stage. Check that you do understand. This is the most important stage, so be prepared to spend most time at it.	Concentrate on your *underlying* feelings. Ask your partner to check out with you to see if (s)he has grasped what you are saying.
T.V.	*Husband:* The reason we don't have a colour T.V. is because you spend money as if it was going out of fashion!	*Wife:* (summing up as husband talks). You'd love to buy a new television and you're annoyed because I don't save money . . . You've a sense of having no control when the money seems to disappear . . . It's frustrating for you.	*Wife:* This may be difficult for you to listen to but I would like to help you understand my feelings. I would like a new T.V.. too, but I feel trapped and hemmed in by a budget . . . I find it awfully difficult to be tied down like this.
SEX	*Wife:* What about treating me as a person for a change! Do you never think of anything else but sex!	*Husband:* (summing up as wife talks) You often feel confused and hurt when we make love in a hurry, because you would like to spend a while just chatting first. . . it takes you a while to warm up. You hate making love without that time to chat first . . .	*Husband:* I feel terribly small and humiliated when I always seem to be the one who suggests making love. It's a very unequal situation — like a little dog that has to beg for my food. I often wish I didn't need you because it's so horrible to feel this way.

3. What we'd like.	4. Brainstorm.	5. Choose a solution.	6. Plan the details.
Allow ourselves to dream a little bit. What would the ideal situation be? Forget about being practical or realistic for a little while.	Any ideas that might help. Agree not to discuss suggestions or to look at snags until you have got as many ideas as possible down on paper.	Look at the advantages of each possibility until you agree on one.	Make your plans as specific as possible. Also fix a definite time for reviewing how things are going.
Husband: I would love not to have to worry about bills. To have enough money to buy all the things we need and to have some savings. *Wife:* I would just love to have the simple pleasure of being able to buy things without always feeling guilty.	Maybe we should: (A) Do part-time work / overtime. (B) Put aside a small sum each week? (C) Rent a T.V.? (D) Borrow money?	We agree that we have borrowed enough money — and we're not really interested in extra work. We eventually decide to put a little money aside each week.	Down to specifics. How much money can we realistically save without feeling too tied or crippled? When will we buy the T.V.? Are we definitely prepared to do this? We'll see how our plan is working out, in two week's time.
Wife: I'd love to be cuddled and loved and chatted to, to be noticed and to be special to you all day before we make love. *Husband:* I'd love you to need me, to suggest making love more often. I'd like us to be relaxed and free with each other, even to make love at unusual times.	Some possibilities might be: (A) Plan to make love from morning time? (B) Come to bed earlier when we want to make love? (C) Put on music and create the right mood?	A and C are out because one partner is unhappy about planning love-making and finds that chatting seems to be the only way that helps to create the right mood. We decide to come to bed earlier.	Let's come to bed at least half an hour earlier when we are going to make love. Are we both happy with this decision? Let's sit down again at the end of the month to see how things are going.

CASE STUDIES (Alternative to listening to the cassette tapes)

1. Form groups of three (or couples, if you came as a couple). Tell each other which of the six 'stages' in Table Three you consider most important? Why do you think that? Please respect those who think differently to you.

2. Tick any of the following areas which cause tension in your relationship, and underline the two or three which cause most tension. Then share with one another what you marked. How would you feel about using the six stages in Table Three for talking to your partner about one of these tensions? It's best to start small - so which of the areas below might be a good one to start with? How might you start with li .ening?

AREAS OF TENSION:

How much television to watch, and what programmes.
In-laws, mine, yours, visits, responsibilities, interference...
Children (parenting, discipline, worries, education, friends, health).
Money and how I/ you spend it (or save it).
Sex (too much, too little, when, where, preparation). Family planning.
Time, or the lack of it - mine, yours, demands.
Sport - and leisure. How we spend evenings, weekends, holidays.
What I'd really like to do in life - education, career, ambition.
Feminism, and male/ female roles.
Where we live. Feelings about house, neighbourhood, community..
God, church, prayer, my/ your faith, my/ your involvement...
Work in and around the house.
Friends - mine, yours, ours, tensions, attractions, jealousies.
What would happen if one of us died.
Communication, or the lack of it, in our marriage.
Health - food, tablets, drinking, smoking, worries about health...
My work, your work, unemployment, fears, overworking...
Voluntary work, organisations I/ you belong to.
Lifestyle, mine, yours, pressures, dissatisfactions...

The topics above are powerful areas for deepening communication and building a relationship. It is always possible to come back to them, share your feelings, and discuss them long after a course has finished.

LISTENING EXERCISE

Below are some signs of good listening. During the exercise, observe the listener to see how many you notice (bearing in mind that many people also experience good listening when some of these signs are absent).

___Silent most of the time

___Not joking, reassuring or 'consoling'

___Looked at speaker (without staring)

___Not offering advice or suggestions

___Caring and understanding face/eyes

___Repeated occasional word/ phrase

___Helpful 'yes', 'uh-huh', 'I see...'

___Body position helpful

___Tone of voice encouraging

___Reflected back feelings

___Helpful nod or gesture

___Did not ask questions

___Anything else?

___Overall impression

PLANS FOR NEXT WEEK

Here are a few more topics for practising active listening during the week. Allow your partner to speak for three to five minutes without interruption; then say briefly in your own words what you heard - especially the feelings. Next it's your turn to talk. If anything difficult crops up, it may be best to postpone talking about it until a suitable time when you can go through the six stages of problem-solving. The following are the suggested topics for your chats. It would be great if you could manage them all, but do make sure to set aside time for at least one of them.

1. Who was angry with me/cruel towards me as a child? Tell the story.
2. A serious row we had - not too recently! How I thought and felt then.
3. Am I happy with the way I'm living? What are my chief tensions or frustrations at present? What would I like to change?
4. My biggest problem at present.
5. How was my day today? - what I did, what I was thinking, what I felt.
6. Some things I'd like to do with my life, if I had the chance. What needs do I think I have that lie beneath these desires?

For next week it is also suggested that you try going through the six stages of problem-solving with one minor problem. It might be something like planning a day's outing, a problem with one of the children, buying someone's wedding present, getting something in the house mended... Or it may be something which crops up during your ten minute chat. Remember that it is best to practise with minor problems first. And do keep up the encouragement.

TIPS FOR GETTING ALONG BETTER

● Money, sex, in-laws, work, leisure time, all tend to be major areas of conflict in a marriage — but also the areas that may lead to the greatest growth. So it may be important not to avoid these topics, but to tell your partner how you feel and to discover how (s)he feels. That has helped many couples to get along much better together and to find much greater fulfilment in their marriage.

● *See if you can postpone dealing with problems until a time that suits you both. Not too late at night — and when you've calmed down a little bit.*

● If you own the problem, that is, if you are the one most upset by it, try giving an I-message: 'I feel so frustrated I could cry when I go to so much trouble getting a meal ready and then you don't come in when I call you.'; 'When I come in from work and you want to talk to me and tell me all about your day, I feel a bit battered because I seem to need about half an hour to recover and to change gear.': 'I feel miles from you when you treat me like that because I get the impression that you're only interested in my body, and that's humiliating for me.'

● *If your partner owns the problem, i.e. if (s)he is the one most upset by it, active listening is the best starting point: 'You're very annoyed with the children because they went off without cleaning up and without saying where they were going.' But don't expect someone with strong feelings to calm down immediately. When you use active listening, their anger may get worse initially before they begin to calm down Indeed, silent listening may be best when your partner is angry with you, because anything you say can so easily be misinterpreted by an angry person — whereas your silence can actually help them to become aware of their own feelings.*

● For bigger problems, try the six stages of problem-solving — see Table Three. Don't let yourself get bogged down with the mechanics of getting all the stages in the right order, but some kind of structure is usually essential if you are to resolve difficulties effectively, peacefully and with respect for each other. If you do blow your top occasionally, of course, that may do no harm — it may even help to clear the air — but you might take the first opportunity to say sorry.

● *Some suggestions for having a constructive row are: Find out what your argument is really about and stick to the point. No name-calling. Don't rake up past history ('You did the same thing at Christmas two years ago!') Leave other people out of it ('You're just like your mother!'). Finish the row - it's unfair to burst into tears and run off slamming the door behind you. It may also help to give each other a hug or some sign of making up after a row. It is especially helpful to make up before you go to bed so that you can make a fresh start in the morning.*

COMMENTS
AND
REACTIONS

"I don't know. Going through those stages is okay, I suppose. But it mightn't suit some people. What about a blow-up? If we have a row and we come through it as friends, isn't that fine! My husband and I gave up playing scrabble because I threw the board at him for being too 'clever'. And I would still throw it — I wouldn't have the patience for working through a problem that way!"

"I'd love to be able to go through those stages in Table Three — I have a whole list of things we really need to talk out!"

"We had our first problem-solving session on smoking, and I feel we're making some progress — that's a real 'biggie' in our marriage".

"It's all too serious and boring — like a list of all the right things to do to be able to bear the pain of being married! I'd rather put the emphasis on laughing and having a bit of fun together. I mean, a few days ago I said to my husband "I'll burn those bloody gardening trousers if I see you wearing them again" and we ended up laughing our heads off. But he got the message."

"We're more relaxed with each other and we're now able to talk about difficult areas without flying off the handle."

"It was hard to tell her how much the way she treated the children annoyed me, but, when she checked out that she had understood me, my annoyance actually sounded natural enough, and I felt a great sense of relief."

"It was very easy to listen to him once he began to open up. He was kind of wary at first, then he was more trusting, and when we had finished, he said: 'You know, when you're in a mood like this, I'd rather talk to you than watch TV' That was something from Bill! But it's also paying off in other ways — when I listen to him, I notice he then listens to me better".

"When he came in so late I felt like going on the attack, but instead I decided to give him an I-message. I said: 'Maurice, I was so frightened that something had happened to you. I'm so glad to see you.' And I hugged him. It was *just* the right thing to do — and much better than acting on my feelings. I don't know how I've missed the point for so long... Now I understand better what people mean when they say a marriage needs to be worked at."

CHAPTER 4: LETTING YOUR MARRIAGE GROW

A settled marriage.

Eight years ago, when Ann and David got married, they were crazy about each other. Now they have settled down, have adjusted to living together, and have things pretty well worked out between them. They are faithful to one another and reasonably happy. Recently, however, Ann has begun to feel that something is missing. David likes to talk to her about his work and about the day's news, but she would like more *personal* conversation. She would like to talk about their sex life, for example, but David doesn't see any need — it's okay, he says. Sometimes she has a sense of there being almost no *real* communication between them. When they went on holidays last month, there was a terrible feeling of emptiness and dullness. They seemed to have very little to say to each other. Their marriage seemed to have lost a lot of its excitement and sparkle. Not what Ann had hoped for. Maybe this was the way it had to be?

The problem is this marriage is a very common one. Ann and David have accepted the idea that a couple should 'settle down' when they get married

— you get married, you adjust to each other, you come to working arrangements, and that's it. They don't realise that a healthy marriage never stops growing — as the personality of each partner continues to change and grow. One partner changes, then the other, and some tension results. This is usually dealt with by talking things out and making some changes. And in this way, a marriage, like the partners, stretches and grows, and that helps to make a couple more attractive, more alive, more 'sparky'. Without this growing, a marriage tends to lose its spark and can become a bit boring and dull.

When a couple realise this, and willingly take on the caring and support that allow them both to grow together, they are taking a big step towards building a successful, healthy, happy marriage. Healthy marriages will take many different shapes, of course, but let's look at what one couple looks like in this more alive kind of marriage.

A growing marriage.

Olive and Andrew are married 17 years. For them faithfulness does not mean making suitable working arrangements to ensure they stay together — nor merely staying out of other people's beds; faithfulness means sharing their lives together, being intimate and warm with one another, sharing responsibilities, talking out tensions, spending time together. There are sometimes serious misunderstandings between them, and an occasional row — when Andrew tells Olive what he believes to be the truth at the time, namely that she is one of the most unreasonable people he has ever met, and she tells him to stop lecturing at her and acting so superior. 'In the middle of a row, I feel as if I hate him', Olive says, 'And I don't think I could cope if we didn't know each other so well, if we hadn't spent so much time talking to each other — if we weren't best friends, I suppose.'

For Olive and Andrew have seldom allowed work and children to interfere with their own time together. They see that as their life-line, and you can see the effect in the way they get along. It is obvious that they love each other. They're relaxed with one another, they're usually gentle, and they're warm without being over-sentimental. They enjoy teasing each other. Andrew tells Olive how lucky she is to have got him, that there were lots of other women around who fancied him. Olive tells Andrew she wishes she had got someone without a bald patch, that next time around she'll marry a man with a full head of hair — and one who can hammer nails in straight!

*In the middle of a row
I feel as if I hate him.*

They make a point of going out together about once a week, often just for a walk. 'You can't walk too far without beginning to talk' Andrew claims 'Even if you're hopping mad with each other to start off with.'

Sex, too, is very important for them. 'I think I got married because I love being cuddled', Olive says 'And I still love that about being married. Sex allows us to be unbelievably intimate and close.' Andrew agrees. 'At times there have been bad patches — we've had some awful rows, including rows about sex' she claims, 'But sex has also helped us to mend the rows and make up again.'

The three essentials of a healthy marriage.

It is obvious to those who know Olive and Andrew that they love each other deeply. There is something very relaxed and real and attractive about them. It is hard to put a finger on what it is that is so attractive, but they would certainly appear to have the three basics for a healthy marriage. 1. Their marriage has not stopped growing and changing — they want to go on growing together and encouraging each other's growth. 2. They communicate openly and regularly — so there is a great deal of honesty and trust between them. 3. They do not run away from difficulties; they

55

talk about their differences and their disagreements, and they grow through them.

These three things — keeping on growing, communicating effectively, and dealing well with disagreements — are what Dr. David Mace describes as the three essentials for a healthy, happy marriage and the secret of success for married couples. He came to this conclusion after a life-time of working with many different kinds of marriages in Europe, Africa, the United States, and Australasia, and after studying marriage in all the major human cultures. His recipe can be summed up in three words: growing through communication.

Improving Communication.

Now it is easy to trot out a word like communication. Everyone seems to agree on its importance. But what exactly does it involve, and why is effective communication lacking in so many marriages?

The fact is that many couples have reasonably good communication, but they do not realise how much *more* is possible. In the first example, David talked about his work and the day's news; yet Ann was very dissatisfied with the lack of personal conversation. So it is quite possible to talk a lot about friends, children, work, neighbours, little scraps of news, ideas and so on — and all this is good — but there is much more. Talking about feelings can make a big difference. It is easy to take your partner for granted and assume you know what is happening to them until they surprise you with their feelings. This is one of the great advantages in taking a few uninterrupted minutes each to talk about what has been happening to you and what has been going on inside you during the day. Many couples find it sheer luxury to have that short period of guaranteed listening time every day.

That brings us to a second thing which could improve communication dramatically. Many people think communication is about talking; whereas it is much more about *listening*. This is probably very obvious to anyone who has done this course, because the emphasis on each evening has been on active listening and understanding. Many marriage counsellors consider that active listening is the single most essential skill for a healthy, growing, fulfilling marriage. Again, special times for uninterrupted chatting offer a great opportunity for practising this skill as well as for growing in closeness and intimacy.

Communication through touch.

And a third reason for the lack of better communication between couples is that many of them do not realise the importance of the communication that takes place without words. As we saw in the first chapter, we communicate much more by what we don't say, by how we look at one another, by our body positions, by how we raise an eyebrow or lock our arms — and by how we touch. Before marriage, young couples say so much to each other by how they touch, they express their desires, their caring, their tenderness, even with the lightest touch of a finger against a finger. Many of them envy married couples who can share their entire lives and bodies. For sex *is* a powerful way for a couple to communicate their love for each other, their trust, their caring. There can be so much communication in the cuddling, the excitement, and the intimate touching of sharing a home and a bed.

In our society, unfortunately, so much emphasis has been put on physical sex, on 'it', on mutual climax, and so on — and so little emphasis on sex as a way of communicating. The impression of sex that tends to be 'just right' as a couple fall into bed is reinforced by films, T.V., books and magazines — and that can do a lot of harm. The fact is that a couple who can snuggle close together and communicate to each other that they have no sexy feelings at all may have quite a good sexual relationship — precisely because they're able to communicate together as man and woman. Indeed how to make contact without inevitably ending in sexual intercourse is an important stage of the growth of a marriage. There are no rules for good sex, of course, and there is no ideal sexual relationship. But it does help many people to think of sex as a way of communicating rather than as a mere physical activity.

But, but, but...

All this points to the importance of open communication for a happy marriage. But is it not a bit artificial to have to plan time to talk together? Should communication not be something that happens without planning? Well, of *course* there will be a certain amount of communication without planning, but in today's pressured world, many people confess that they can be so busy with work, children, and so on, that days, even weeks, can go by when they scarcely meet as persons. They feel the need for a certain amount of structure and planning to make sure that they have time together in the midst of all their pressures. And marriage support programmes throughout the world point to couples taking a few short minutes talking and a few short minutes listening as a simple but very powerful way of providing that.

Couples sometimes say that they don't wish to live in each other's pockets, that they feel a great need to fight for and guard their personal space and

They feel a great need to fight for and guard their personal space and freedom.

freedom. This objection is very proper. Each one's freedom and space need to be respected. But many people who work with couples also remind us that real intimacy between husband and wife actually *increases* their freedom. Indeed, the better a couple's communication is, the more each one's personality can develop. Every couple is different, of course, so you need to find your own balance, at the same time watching for the growth of that invisible wall which shuts you off from each other.

But what if one partner doesn't want to talk? What if (s)he is just not interested? In that case, it can help to ask *why* (s)he is not interested? Sometimes women are so pleased to get their husbands talking to them that they make the mistake of extending the length of their special chatting time — which can be a real turn-off to a husband. However, this may also be an area where the stages for dealing with conflict can be used effectively — you may need to be very real with your partner and talk about your frustration. Remember that the effective use of anger and conflict is one of the three essentials for a healthy marriage. But do be gentle, and don't push or force the issue, if you want to be effective.

Finding fulfilment in marriage.

Some of the ideas in this chapter and in this course may seem strange. Our parents didn't have all these awarenesses and skills, so how did they manage, you may ask. It is important, then, to recognise that marriage is under a great deal more pressure today than in the past. There are more distractions, it is easier to escape — and people now expect a lot more from marriage. They expect equality, personal growth, fulfilment, happiness, better communication. They are right to expect these things, and they are all possible.

For the fact is that marriage today can be deeply fulfilling in a way that previous generations could not have imagined. There is probably no better way to support the growth of your partner's personality and at the same time to change yourself for the better, than to develop the art of married listening that allows your marriage to become alive and growing. Regular communication constantly raises the level of trust, renews the marriage, and helps you to go on surprising each other. With effective communication, marriage now offers great new possibilities, not only for personal growth, but also for growing in understanding and closeness and for growing in love.

GETTING IN TOUCH: PLANNING FOR A BETTER MARRIAGE

Here are six suggestions for improving a marriage which people have found helpful. Decide how you think you are doing at present — and what you would most like for the future.

	How you're doing Mark 1st, 2nd & 3rd for the things you are best at (in that order).	What you'd like Mark 1st, 2nd & 3rd for the things you would most like for your marriage.
1. **Open Communication** — time each day for listening and talking together — or a few regular times each week.		
2. **Time Out** — time to go out together, perhaps once a week. To a film, for a drink, or just simply for a walk...		
3. **Deal with problems** — Postpone dealing with problems until suitable time. Use some structure, including active listening, for resolving conflict.		
4. **Regular encouragement** — On the lookout for the good in your partner and reflecting it naturally and often.		
5. **Group support** — an occasional retreat, a regular support-group meeting, a course for couples...		
6. **Seeking help** — looking for help from qualified counsellors before problems get out of hand.		

TABLE 4: FIFTEEN MINUTES TOGETHER

The table below is based on what many couples do regularly (in many cases a few times a week, sometimes daily) to keep their communication open. You will obviously adapt it to your own circumstances — which could even mean listening without your partner being aware that this is a special form of communication. Either way, your partner will usually be very appreciative, for this method of communication is generally very enjoyable, and can quickly become part of your way of life.

1. **Make the time.** Set aside ten to fifteen minutes that will be free from interruptions. Preferably not too late in the evening or you may be too tired.
2. **Listen.** Allow your partner to speak for five minutes without interruption — about whatever seems important to him/her. Make a conscious decision to love — to switch off your own concerns and listen to your partner's feelings, especially feelings that (s)he may not even mention.
3. **Summing up.** Next, take a minute to sum up in your own words what you have heard, (especially the feelings), checked out that you have understood. Allow your partner to interrupt you, to explain something in more detail or to clarify what you haven't understood.
4. **Your turn to talk.** Now it's your turn to talk for five minutes about whatever is relevant to you — your thoughts, your plans, whatever is important to you right now. Concentrate mainly on your feelings. Avoid criticism of the other — a gentle I-message is far more effective.
5. **Clarify.** Now allow your partner to sum up what you have said. Feel free to interrupt, to explain, to clarify.
6. **Discuss.** It will sometimes be necessary to take a few more minutes to make plans or to discuss something arising out of your chat together. If a more serious problem has arisen, postpone discussion on it — you can decide together on a time to talk it through. Table Three gives a useful method for dealing with such problems.

CASE STUDIES (Alternative to listening to the cassette tapes)

1. Read Table Four, then form pairs, and explain to each other how the 'Fifteen minutes together' works. (When you have to explain something, that often helps you to understand it better.)

2. Take a few minutes to discuss the following situation:
Jean has attended this course without her husband, Tom. When she comes home on the last evening, he laughs at her efforts, 'Oh, it's you. You've been out with those silly women again. Have they told you how to change me yet?'
Can you think of ways in which Jean might stay friendly and use active listening or a sincere I-message? How would you handle this situation without being aggressive - or apologetic?

COMMENTS
AND
REACTIONS

"This course has stopped me in my tracks and given me far more than I had hoped for. When I started I felt bogged down by a number of things — children, work, and so on. I just didn't think about my marriage. Now everything seems better, and other things have fallen into place. I'm very grateful."

"There's too much emphasis on making time to talk together. Don't get me wrong — I'm all for more communication — but it doesn't have to be as intense as all that. It drives me crazy when my wife wants to be too close. You need to allow for people to have time and space on their *own*. Besides, I don't want to know everything about my wife. I like to keep some of the mystery — you need a bit of space."

"Mary hated our new house as soon as she moved in. I tried every argument I could think of, with no success. Eventually I listened. Really listened. It was then I realised that what she was going through was very like what I had suffered as a child. No way did I want to force her to stay in the house any longer. We started looking for a new one. But the extraordinary thing is that we didn't need to move. Just being listened to solved the problem for Mary, and she's completely settled now."

"The course has reminded me of how good our marriage used to be, and it has made me want to kindle that again."

"Great laughs! And great learning! I looked forward to each Tuesday, and I felt really supported by everyone. This is the kind of community and the kind of support people are crying out for."

"I don't know. The programme didn't mean very much to me. The only thing that was new was the religious dimension — I had never seen a connection between God and my marriage."

"My biggest regret is that my husband didn't do the course with me."

"A lot of things have come up for Derek and me that we might never have got around to talking about. It's a whole new way to communicate."

"That kind of artificial set-up is for the birds, not for the real world, with all the pressures and tensions and pulls of lifting and laying kids and coping with work and friends and the house. We hardly *meet* some days."

"I got what I wanted from the course. I got a way of keeping our marriage alive and growing, and my listening has improved. We've been using the daily ten minutes together now for the past year and a half."

TIPS FOR GETTING ALONG BETTER

● The three essentials for a healthy marriage are commitment to growth, effective communication and dealing well with disagreements. In three words: growth through communication.

● *The more time and effort and patience you put into your marriage, the more you will tend to get out of it. After all, love is more than a mere feeling; it is a decision, especially a decision to listen in a deeper, more tender, non-defensive way — to use active listening. Many marriage support programmes suggest that couples set aside ten to fifteen minutes to do this a few times a week.*

● A sense of humour is a great help to a marriage — provided your partner appreciates your sense of fun! Humour can also be an effective way of dealing with tension at times, but it should not be used as an escape from facing conflict and talking it through — you may need to put aside an occasional half hour and use some suitable structure to deal with an area of conflict.

● *It is important to take time to become aware of your partner's goodness — and to let them know what you have noticed. If your partner and your marriage are to grow, encouragement is the sunshine that enables that growth to take place.*

● It is useful to think of sex as a way of communicating rather than a physical activity. In fact, sex for many couples is as good or as bad as their general level of communication. Talking about your feelings about sex, even your lack of sexual feeling, can also help.

● *Married couples who seek to improve their marriages often find themselves swimming against the current of modern society. Some form of group support — and sometimes a visit to a good marriage counsellor — can prove extremely helpful. Don't wait to seek help until your marriage is breaking down. Counselling can work wonders for a marriage if you have the maturity and the good sense to seek it before the problems get out of hand. Many happily married couples claim that they owe their happiness to a marriage counsellor whom they approached in time.*

● Have you ever noticed how renewing it is to go out together for an evening — forgetting about children, work and problems as you watch a film or go for a walk together. Very often a couple would like this time together but it doesn't happen because they fail to plan it.

● *Table Four gives an outline for a simple technique that has helped many thousands of couples to keep in touch and to deepen their love. It is not going to solve all your problems, of course, and no one technique is suitable for everyone, but it is worth trying.*

EVALUATION

Just answer the questions where you feel you have something to say, and give the completed form to the person who ran your course — it will help them to adapt and improve things for the next people who do the course.

1. Please mark 1st, 2nd and 3rd the parts of the evening you liked most (in that order) and mark x for any part of the evening you disliked.

    Sharing of how we got on since last week.
    Discussion based on the Table.
    Listening to the situations on the tape.
    The listening practice in twos and threes.
    The reflections read at the end.
    The social side — chatting afterwards over the cup of tea.

2. What did you like about the course or learn during it?

3. What disappointed you about the course?

4. What would have made the course better?

5. What effect (if any) has the course had on you or on your marriage? (In what ways do you think your outlook or approach has changed?)

FURTHER SUPPORT

Many people want follow-up after completing this course, and some form of follow-up is very much to be encouraged.

The ideal follow-up is probably something which reinforces the skills which people have just learnt. The simplest thing may be just to do this course a second time. For example, some of the groups who have experienced our parenting programme continue to meet to go through that course again — and many of them claim that they get much more out of it the second time around. Their meetings usually take the same format as the course itself — but possibly leaving out the tapes and basing the discussion for that part of the session on the Tips or Comments at the end of each chapter, or on problems surfaced from the group. The original leaders do not have to belong to this ongoing support group; it often happens that a different person takes responsibility for running each session, so that the leadership is revolved and more people involved.

For parents, another suggested follow-up might be the Basic Parenting Programme, or the Teen-Parenting Programme, if they have not experienced these courses. These parenting programmes also provide parents with an opportunity to reinforce the same skills.

And another possibility, which has already been mentioned, is to run the course, with a little adaptation, for those *couples* who are open to it. Couples are encouraged, too, to try a Marriage Enrichment Weekend or a Marriage Encounter Weekend and to consider taking part in any follow-up activites provided after these Weekends. Marriage Encounter Weekends are normally organised by churches, and the address will usually be found in the church directory. Information about Marriage Enrichment may be obtained from: Association for Marriage Enrichment, Westminster Pastoral Foundation, 23 Kensington Square, London W8 5HN.

COURSE GUIDELINES

Those taking part in this programme are asked to consider the following guidelines.

1. Take it seriously. We hope you will find this course very enjoyable, as most people do, but you are also asked to take it seriously. It is important, for example, to come to all four sessions, and to practise the skills during the week, for each session builds on the one before it. Those who work hard at the skills between sessions tend to see a great improvement in their marriages.

2. Play your part. Some people are naturally shy and reluctant to speak, even in a small group. No one at any stage has to talk in the group, but talking things out together can help both you and the others, so the more open you can be the better — you have much more to offer than you may think.

3. Give the others a chance. This guideline is for the person who tends to talk too much. Please don't speak a second time about any topic until everyone has at least had an opportunity to speak once. Hogging the conversation is just not fair to the others. If you tend to overtalk, it will really help you personally to draw others out and encourage them to talk first.

4. Respect people's confidences. During the course, it may happen that members of the group will trust you by telling you personal things about themselves. If so, it is important to respect that trust and not to talk about such matters outside the group.

5. Take it slowly. Don't let discouragement beat you if you make mistakes or seem to be slow about getting results. Learning new skills takes time and patience — you know what it's like learning to cook, to ride a bike, to type, or to play a musical instrument. 'Little and often' is the golden rule for picking up new skills. And it's certainly not a good idea to arrive home 'high' after a session and try everything out on a tired partner.

6. What works for you. You're not expected to use or to agree with everything on this course. Many couples already have a very good relationship and are not using these skills — we're all different. But you are asked to respect that difference in others too. People have a right to their own approach and their own opinion. What works for you may not work for them, so feel free to say what works for you but please don't advise others or criticise them.

7. No partner bashing! Please do not use this group to criticise your partner. This is a positive, marriage-building support group. It is also a fundamental principle of the course that the only person you can change is yourself; your partner and your family can begin to change when you do. In fact, one of the best ways to free people to change is to show them respect and understanding, and not to pass judgement on them.